ANGELS IN THE 21ST CENTURY

CENTURY

A NEW PERSPECTIVE ON DEATH AND DYING

SONJA GRACE

ANGELS IN THE 21ST CENTURY

Published by Market House Books
Seattle, WA

First Edition
Library of Congress Control Number 2010920210

ISBN 978-0-944638-55-2
Cover photograph by Shawn Sockyma

TO MY HUSBAND SHAWN

Mission Statement for Humanity

The mission statement for humanity is to love at the deepest level of your being. The work we have to do here on Earth is to feel our feelings. There is a karmic solution to the earthly experience of feeling one's feelings and loving at the deepest level of one's being. The Karmic solution is to forgive.

Love, feel, forgive - that is the human experience

When we are truly in our authentic self these components (loving, feelings, forgiveness) are possible and very much available to us all the time. How we choose to experience death is up to us. We can let life happen to us, remaining victims to karmic situations we actually created life times ago, or we can take responsibility for our lives.

We can claim knowledge to clear karma and, in so doing, face the experience of being a soul in a body here on earth as the core statement to our self-worth.

We have much work to do while we are here. Knowledge of the past can help create the present; it can shape our future so the process called life can prepare us for the greatest passage of all:

DEATH

INTRODUCTION

My earliest memory of seeing the spirit realm was as a child of five years old. I was born with gifts that were far beyond my comprehension. At twelve I watched the entire spirit realm walk through my bedroom.

Thanks to my parents, who did the only logical thing parents could do, I was channeled into the arts and received classical ballet training that catapulted me into a rich professional career spanning a decade at the prestigious Oregon Shakespeare Festival. I gained understanding for my gifts when I sat in front of my first teacher. She helped me ground and create a platform for my abilities.

Angels in the 21st Century was born out of the idea that as a healer and spiritual intuitive there is a place for mystics like me in this world. For over 30 years I have worked with people around the globe offering immediate stability, clarity and guidance.

All of my work comes through communicating and channeling the Divine. The guides and angels that work with me are the very essence of a personal history. I know that I have lived multiple lifetimes working as a healer, mystic, clairvoyant, psychic and spiritual intuitive.

I see, smell, hear and feel the spirit realm. Because of my experience as a spiritual intuitive, I am able to access information to help clients that I work with. Clients call me for an assortment of reasons, including depression, death of a loved one, illness (themselves or a family member), marriage, divorce, business, childhood issues, love... and much more.

The one topic that comes up time and again is death. People are eternally interested in one's own (or a loved one's) passing in either this or a past life. The major point of reference we all share usually springs from a religious affiliation that we might have grown up with. Many people find themselves wrestling with belief systems that are out-dated; that just don't work for them anymore. For this reason, I have included various religious perspectives on death so that there is a reference point from which to begin. Religion throughout cultures has influenced our views on death in particular. We often share a much different experience with death through out history based on the religious framework of an earlier time.

I view death and dying as a completion of ones work here on Earth. It is an incredible journey and we all make it. We have the earthly experience of being alive in a body, feeling our feelings, and loving at the deepest level of our beings. This is the reason we are here. But beyond all of this we must also work through our karma. Karma is the wonderful library of experience that hasn't been quite resolved and is a legacy challenge from our past lives. Naturally, we are back here on Earth to work through what is left unresolved. We all have this opportunity to work through and clear our karma. This is the key to my work and helping others. My path has been filled with many clients who search for their real purpose here on Earth, redefining a connection to this planet that has long been lost.

As we strive towards finding our spiritual place we reconnect with our true nature, and discover a passage that we have all experienced numerous times. I invite you to look into yourself; join me on this journey by seeing a new perspective on death and dying.

THE DYING PROCESS

The funny thing about death is we all have to go through it. It is one of the tried and true passages that each one of us must make and yet it is the very journey no one wants to talk about. For the most part we all take it the wrong way. It is perceived as the end... I will never see them again. People believe an assortment of things concerning where they are going; for instance, heaven, hell, purgatory, the ground, and (my all time favorite) a white cloud while playing a harp and floating in some heavenly space.

These are interesting ideas pertaining to death and the dying process, but we are much more complex than all of that. Our souls have many lives. Belief in reincarnation has ancient roots. This doctrine is a central tenet within the majority of Indian religious traditions, such as Hinduism (including Yoga, Vaushnavism, and Shaivism) and Jainism. In early Greece, many philosophers understood this idea also and from past history through to the present day it is possible to get many diverse narratives about what it means to die. And indeed, depending on a person's culture or persuasion, there are many perspectives on death. Below are samples of how some individuals perceive the journey and process of death and dying. The perspective of some deep-seated religious bodies is described briefly here, including Christians, Islamists, Hindus, Buddhists and Jews. You might see some similarities among the beliefs of these diverse ethnic and religious peoples and yet great differences.

A CHRISTIAN PERSPECTIVE

The Christian grief process is generally guided by scripture from the bible because there are statements such as, "There is a time to be born, and a time to die." This gives believers the knowledge that we all have our time. For Christians, death is a part of life and many Christians believe that it is their duty to take care of the dying as they wait for Jesus to return. Christians have a wide variety of beliefs after death, but most believe that death is just another part of the journey as we all experience eternal life so long as one believes in Jesus Christ.

AN ISLAMIC PERSPECTIVE

In the Islamic faith, grief is something that involves the person dying as well as those around him or her. When someone is dying in this faith, it is the job of the friends and family to gather around the ill person and help them remember their commitment to God. Muslims believe that death is the will of Allah. After death the body is washed and wrapped in a shroud. There are specific prayers that are to be said and the body is to be laid on the right side facing the direction of Makkah. In the Islamic faith the family members are to pay off any debts of the deceased soon after death as they anticipate the person being judged after death and want the process to be as favorable as possible. Bereavement in this faith is often accompanied by constant prayer, charity, fasting, and pilgrimage.

AN HINDU PERSPECTIVE

Many people have commented over the ages that grief management seems a lot easier for the people of this faith. While this may or may not be true, it could be owed to the fact that those that practice this religion believe in the rebirth as well as the reincarnation of souls. Practitioners believe that death is simply part of the experience, and that after a time the soul will adjust and return to physical form again. There are two paths for the soul to take after death; the path of the sun and the path of the moon. Those that take the path of the sun will never return again but those that take the path of the moon will return. Many different rituals have been practiced for thousands of years and may help with the grief process.

A BUDDHIST PERSPECTIVE

The Buddhist perspective of death is quite interesting and is said to make grief not so troublesome for those that have suffered a loss. The practitioners of this faith do not look at death as a sad event, rather the breaking apart from the material world and material that we are composed of. A Buddhist believes that the soul awakens at death. Before the death friends and family like to be with the person to help them achieve the right state of mind as they go into death. One needs to think of death as their rebirth into another, and perhaps greater, realm than the human world can offer.

A JEWISH PERSPECTIVE

Not unlike Christians, those that are Jewish tend to view death as a natural experience. Many Jewish people believe that death gives life more meaning and that because we know we all must die sometime, we should spend each day living the more pure and ethical life possible. Unlike a lot of faiths, Judaism is a bit different in that they don't believe that all believers will simply go to Heaven or Hell based on their belief or lack thereof. Instead, individuals will be judged on their ethical behavior during life. For this reason, Jewish people view death as natural but their final judgment by God.[1]

> To think we come here but once is to limit the very nature of what our souls are.

A NEW LOOK AT DEATH

If we look at death through the four essential bodies we will have a better understanding for the process and passage that we make. The four essential bodies are detailed here.

◇ The physical body is what we experience everyday we are alive. Consider these emotions... my body feels good, my body feels bad, my body has an illness, my body needs to work out.

◇ The mental body is our experience of the mind and our ability to process information.
◇ The emotional body is what we are feeling. Through our experience of being in bodies we are given the opportunity to process those feelings.
◇ The spiritual body is our soul, which is housed in our physical body. Our spiritual body has access to the physical, emotional and mental realms.

These four bodies allow us a daily experience of feeling the physical, emotional and understanding on the mental so that it can be expressed through the spiritual.

FOUR ESSENTIAL BODIES

These four essential bodies—physical, mental, emotional, and spiritual—are constantly aligning and realigning to keep us in balance. We are often out of balance in our four essential bodies, so examining each part in relationship to the death passage will help bring clarity and a deeper understanding. The purpose in doing so will allow for a different perspective on death; where we are going and why. We have lost the fun in making this passage as it has been interpreted as such a dark, sad and morose journey.

My own experience with clients who have family members and loved ones on the other side has revealed a different message. The spirits who come through and want to be heard and share their message of love and or forgiveness are very happy to be on the other side and make comments about not being in pain anymore. They also talk about being immersed in a love that is so profound it is indescribable.

DEATH IN DIFFERENT CULTURES

Many cultures have recorded death journeys throughout history and there is much to be discovered in this passage from this life. In the next few sections we will take a general view of how these cultures deal with grief and the passage to the other world.

AFRICA

In some religions of Africa, life does not end with death, but continues in another realm. The concepts of "life" and "death" are not mutually exclusive concepts, and there are no clear dividing lines between them. Human existence is a dynamic process involving the increase or decrease of "power" or "life force," of "living" and "dying," and there are different levels of life and death.

Death, although a dreaded event, is perceived as the beginning of a person's deeper relationship with all of creation, the complementing of life and the beginning of the communication between the visible and the invisible worlds. The goal of life is to become an ancestor after death. This is why every person who dies must be given a "correct" funeral, supported by a number of religious ceremonies. If this is not done, the dead person may become a wandering ghost, unable to "live" properly after death and therefore a danger to those who remain alive. It might be argued that "proper" death rites are more a guarantee of protection for the living than to secure a safe passage for the dying. There is ambivalence about attitudes to the recent dead, which fluctuate between love and respect on the one hand and dread and despair on the other, particularly because it is believed that the dead have power over the living.

INDIA

In India "death in the midst of life" is a literal, not figurative, notion. Along the Ganges River, for instance, bodies are regularly cremated, and the odor of burning flesh fills the air. And in the city of Calcutta, dead bodies become a problem to those responsible for keeping the streets clean. Thus, it is not surprising that in India's sacred texts and stories, how one lives one's life determines one's fate after death.

What Hinduism offers with regard to death and afterlife is thus not a final decision that must be made in one's present lifetime, but a process that leads through many cycles of death and rebirth until one is able to reach the goal of liberation.

Typically, as a Hindu approaches death, he or she is surrounded with religious rites and ceremonies that support the dying person. Before a Hindu dies, the eldest son and relatives put water taken, if possible, from the Ganges River into the dying person's mouth. At this time, family and friends sing devotional prayers and chant Vedic mantras (sacred sounds). More than the words, which are themselves comforting, the tone of the communal chanting soothes the dying person and comforts relatives in their time of stress and grief.[2]

PLANETARY VIEW

The reflection between Earth and humans is organic. As we move out of our natural state we create imbalance. What was considered a natural state for humans has become messy, dirty, too much trouble, hard to handle and scary for modern man. There are implications. Earth is in balance with us humans. When we are ill she reflects illness as well. We know that earth's climate has changed throughout history. Just in the last 650,000 years there have been seven cycles of glacial advance and retreat, with the abrupt end of the last ice age (about seven thousand years ago), the modern climatic era emerged—and with it, human civilization. Most of these changes are attributed to very small adjustments in earth's orbit; adjustments, which change the amount of direct energy, we receive from the sun. The current warming trend is of particular significance because most of it is very likely human-induced and proceeding at a rate that is unprecedented in the past 1,300 years.[3]

CYCLES OF LIVING AND DYING

Our passage into the next world is natural and so is the Earth in all its glory. If we look at the parallel between Earth and humans we might be surprised by what is right in front of us. There are cycles through out the year that are identified as the seasons in which we experience mini deaths and the renewal of spring.

Elizabeth Kubler-Ross observed that the best way to prepare for your eventual dying is to meet with consciousness the "little deaths" life continually provides.[4] When you are actually in the process of dying, you will be in Autumn's rhythm. Each cycle of completion, each "little death," each autumn in your own life's flow is an opportunity to glean the lessons of the cycle that is ending, to create a meaningful completion, and to open the way for whatever is next to come. Each cycle trains you for all of the autumns yet to be. So it is when your own children leave the nest. So it will be when your body comes to its final season.[5] This is all reflected to us so we might better understand our own journey. The earth has a built-in system to guide us through the year and help us with our own timing as we grow and bring forth children and watch them grow.

Fall is a centerpiece in this respect. When leaves die and descend from the tree we often celebrate the equinox and the changing year. We do this in many different but similar ways throughout the world. In Korea for instance, Chuseok is a major harvest festival and a three-day holiday celebrated around the Autumnal Equinox. This is a form of celebrating the death passage, through what might be experienced as mini-deaths.

CHINA

In China also, people celebrate this time of year with special rituals. The Mid-Autumn festival is celebrated on the 15th day of the 8th lunar month, oftentimes near the autumnal equinox, and is an official holiday. As the lunar calendar is not synchronous with the Gregorian calendar, this date could be anywhere from mid-September to early October.

In the next section we will focus our attention on a concept that is often mysterious and difficult for people to accept and understand. It is, however, a very important aspect of the death passage.

KARMA

Karma refers to the total effect of a person's actions and conduct during the successive phases of that person's existence, and is regarded as determining a person's destiny.

Destiny is the inevitable fate to which a particular person is destined. This is often referred to as "one's lot." In short, destiny is a predetermined course of events considered as something beyond human power or control.

Karma is a critical element of the living and dying process. The need for acknowledgement and understanding for one's life, be it short or long, is essential to creating a joyful death passage. For what we pass with in our emotional body is what we bring into the next life. Karma is the key aspect to understanding what happens as we journey from lifetime to lifetime. It is represented in many religious traditions with everyday implications for living and dying.

In Buddhism, the law of karma is viewed as naturalistic, akin to the laws of physics. Thus, circumstances of rebirths are not seen as rewards or punishments handed out by a controlling God but are simply the natural results of various good deeds and misdeeds. The cycle of rebirths has involved innumerable lives over many eons, including ones in both sexes, in nonhuman animals, and in other realms. It inevitably involves suffering and continues until all cravings are lost and nirvana is achieved.

Hinduism includes the concept of karma, the idea that the conditions into which one is born are determined by one's conduct in various previous lives. Life on Earth is considered undesirable, and an individual may engage in religious practices in each life until eventually earning release from the cycle of rebirth, losing individuality, and achieving union with the infinite spirit (nirvana).

In Judaism, the Kabala is the body of teaching based on an esoteric interpretation of Hebrew scriptures. It includes reincarnation as a major tenet of its doctrine. Hasidic Jews also include reincarnation in their belief system. Reincarnation refers to the belief that after death the body experiences a rebirth in a new body or form of life.

In Christianity too there is reference to reincarnation. Some groups of early Christians, particularly the Gnostic Christians, believed they would be reincarnated, and some Christians in southern Europe believed in it until the Council of Constantinople in 553 C.E. Others find support for reincarnation in the passage in the New Testament Book of Matthew in which Jesus seems to say that John the Baptist is the prophet Elijah returned.[6]

Karma, therefore is a very important aspect of the dying process. When reviewing ones karma we soon realize that it is the glue that helps us connect our life times with much larger patterns of behavioral experiences. Because it is in the process of clearing one's karma that we are released from spiritual baggage we carry. Only then can we evolve in consciousness. This is important since consciousness is a sense of our personal identity, including our attitudes, beliefs, and sensitivities.[7]

THE PHYSICAL BODY

The physical body is the most profound in our experience of death as it is the very vessel we leave behind. We often experience illness and pain as a result of our passage, but rarely is our passage viewed from the perspective of the question: 'what am I supposed to learn from this.'

Society distributes a high level of victimization when it comes to death. In the past, cultures experienced death organically because people's lives were based on cycles of seasons, stars, sun, and moon. Today's society is different in many ways. For a start, we are predominantly urban instead of rural: we are not driven by the seasonal imperatives of agriculture any more. People are often rushed and busy; barely having time to attend a funeral before the need to return back to work for more. We are also heavily influenced by social conditioning at the behest of various religious institutions that instill certain values about death and dying. This explains why, when we are at the end many people believe that based on their lives and actions, they are either going to heaven or hell.

In dealing with the topics of heaven/hell the usual approach in Christianity is to perceive a series of contrasting criteria. These contrasts veer between punishment and reward, grace and pain, or mercy and justice.

With regard to the doctrine of hell, the dominant approach conceives it in terms of punishment. On this basis, one might expect the doctrine of heaven to focus on the concept of reward. Though the concept of reward plays a significant role in the Christian doctrine of heaven, the primary role is played by the concepts of mercy and grace.[8]

As a consequence, many people find themselves at the end panicked and stricken. People tend to question what they have done during their lives, often asking deep questions of themselves at the end. Did I do it wrong? Am I going some place horrible?

When addressing the physical body we should be mindful of our primary and secondary learning modalities to observe how we are handling the physical realm through these structures.

PRIMARY/SECONDARY LEARNING MODALITIES

In this next section we will focus on determining the learning modality that best fits your learning style so that you will gain a deeper understanding of how the death process will appear to you. Primary and secondary learning modalities describe a practical framework for understanding how we view new concepts and ideas that we learn from our environment.

They have a basis for mental understanding and cognition in neurological and linguistic heuristics. The basic assumption of neuro-linguistic programming is that internal mental processes such as problem-solving, memory, and language consist of visual, auditory, kinesthetic, (and possibly olfactory and gustatory) representations that are activated when people think about, or engage in, problems, tasks, or activities.

Internal sensory representations are constantly being formed and activated in our thoughts and actions. Whether making conversation, talking about a problem, reading a book, kicking a ball, or riding a horse, internal representations have an impact on performance. These techniques generally aim to change behavior through modifying the internal representations, examining the way a person represents a problem, and building desirable representations of alternative outcomes or goals.[9]

We each learn in different ways. It is therefore to our advantage when learning new concepts and ideas to understand the best way that we like to receive knowledge and process that knowledge. For instance, one individual might like to read about something first and then look at it, while another person might like to be shown something to touch first before reading about it. This just means that we are individuals expressing our individual and, probably very personal, learning style.

In my practice, as teacher of children for over thirty years, I have worked with a system of four learning structures that facilitate both processing and understanding. I like to focus on visual, tonal, mental and kinesthetic modalities. Having survived a professional career as a ballerina and a lifetime of dance I found it very effective when teaching children to work from this broad framework. I found that visual learners preferred to see what I was doing in order to copy the movement. Tonal learners connected with music—the sound gave them a deep understanding of step work. On the other hand, mental learners liked to calculate timing, focusing on counts and the number of steps that deepened their understanding of the moment. Meanwhile, kinesthetic learners felt through movement and music, and in my experience, these kinesthetic learners were very often the most gifted of dancers.

Most people have a primary and secondary learning modality. If your primary learning mode is kinesthetic and your secondary learning mode is visual you will have the opportunity to experience your physical departure in death from a feeling place and a deeper understanding to what you're picking up from family and loved ones due to your heightened senses. Your visual learning is often enhanced since you might actually connect with the spirit realm and actually see your relatives standing there waiting for you!

There can be a more difficult side to this learning modality however and you should be aware of the implications. There is a possibility that, at the time of death, you might feel everyone else's pain and not be present for your own crossing. In addition, you might see the spirit realm and not understand what you are seeing. In that case you might miss the opportunity to feel comforted in your passage.

Visually you might see the sadness of your family and friends and decide that life isn't fair; that you shouldn't have to leave at this time. Remember, the quality of your passage is up to you.

Realizing a broader view of the journey, it is easy to see why it is recommended that we prepare for this passage lest we miss the experience of transitioning.

Our physical body is designed to teach us compassion and love. The ultimate experience in the physical form is to love at the deepest level of our beings. The body can create a barrier for people who harbor karmic experiences that, combined with current trends in society, leads to a particular belief system.

Both self-esteem and body-image play a large part throughout our lives and impact the final experience of the physical realm. People spend years wrestling with body image. They struggle with self-concepts that dwell negatively on issues like 'I am too fat' or 'too skinny'; 'too short' or 'too tall'; just 'too ugly'. We compare our insides to other people's outsides. 'I am so big next to her'; 'look at my thighs'; 'my butt is huge'; 'how come her waist is small'; 'I look like an elephant'; 'I am losing my hair'; 'I am old.'

This moves into deeper realms that then affect us emotionally. 'I am not good enough'; 'I don't have what it takes'; 'I am a loser'; 'I am not loved'; 'everyone thinks I am stupid'; 'they hate me'; 'I am wrong'; 'God must hate me.' The influence of these self-images and what our society thinks about each of us has a direct impact on the death experience.

How we process and feel our physical form at the time of crossing depends on many things. Have we done any healing work during our lifetime on the physical, emotional, mental and spiritual bodies? Are we at peace and feel we have had a good life? Consequently, are we ready to move forward?

When experiencing death we have the opportunity to feel that physical body; to be grateful for the time we had so that we can release it. The process can be compromised if drugs (such as morphine) have been administered. Morphine is a commonly used drug during the passage of death. It serves the purpose where pain is concerned, but has however some side effects that can alter one's consciousness during the death process.

The side-effects include dizziness, light-headedness, drowsiness, hallucinations, blurred vision and seizures. One side-effect is pretty common. The dying experience coupled with a drug (like morphine) to ease the pain can cause us to leave our bodies and experience the astral plane. This astral plane is outside our world—a planetary sphere that is crossed by the soul in its astral body on the way to being born, and after death. It is described as being populated by angels, spirits, or other immaterial beings.

The result is that we miss the physical experience. However, when it comes to pain one might have little choice. If we trusted that we are in fact going somewhere great (our lives would go on) would the physical departure be easier? Probably, yes! We would find many people experiencing a physical death much quicker and with less fear.

We are extremely attached to the physical and identify with who we are by our appearance. The passage from the physical realm could be a whole new experience if we could embrace the simple knowledge that the death passage is not the end; that we go on to incarnate again and again, each time redefining who we are throughout time.

Reincarnation is a concept that many people have difficulty understanding. However, this idea is widespread and central to many religious denominations.

In Buddhist teachings, sentient beings incarnate due to psychological factors—clinging and ignorance, which result in the phenomenon of becoming and rebirth. To be born human is considered the ultimate privilege because, unlike other mammals, even a person of average intelligence (with sufficient effort and proper guidance) can walk the path of dharma to become liberated from the cycle of rebirth. The motive force in the process of material incarnation is attachment to, and identification with, matter. Ignorance gives rise to volitional factors, which are called sankharas. These sankharas, through infinite possibilities of worldly desires, propel the human being through the pattern of repeated birth and death until a dawning of wisdom (awakening) brings about a desire for liberation.[10]

Our departure can be the opportunity to find this wisdom without attachment. It is our attachment that leads to selfish behavior, which, in turn, can cause suffering for our family and friends. How many people do we know who while crossing over have smiled and said, "I have had a good life and I am ready to go?" Not many!

The common experience is much more self-involved, often displaying hours, months, even years of drama as we patiently wait with family members for our loved one to cross over. The family often experiences great pain while watching a loved one hold on. There is such a difficulty of letting go.

Letting go is a concept that takes us beyond our physical limitations and carries us into trusting the Universe with the knowledge a higher power has our back.

On the first day the new millennium (01.01.01), a good friend of mine recounts how he learned the concept of letting go. It was a hard and difficult lesson; one I share here by way of demonstrating how, even in the most challenging of times, we find deep and abiding lessons about living and dying. Through an expedition to climb Mt. Kenya, where he had hoped to reinvent himself, he describes his moment of transformation.

"It was near the summit when the disaster struck. A climber in another party ahead of us became frostbitten and got stuck in a crux—a challenging overhang. There was nothing for it but a full out rescue. The result was that we were forced to spend the night pinned to the wall a couple pitches below the summit. Without sleep we watching closely the Southern Cross constellation in the ominous African predawn sky. While it was still visible we knew the storm was delayed. Just before sun up the storm broke. Blinding snow and icy winds made it so cold that my glasses glazed over and became unusable. We still had to climb on to the summit before we could rappel the only safe route down.

We prepared the ropes and belays, and tidied up for the descent. Whatever elation I was expecting didn't transpire. Normally, arriving on top of a spectacular equatorial volcano via a two thousand foot vertical basalt spire, which itself was perched high on a fifteen thousand foot crater cone, should have been remarkable and enough to invite this transformation that I desperately sought at the end of a millennial cycle.

I however, was happy to bid adieu to the twin peaks, Nelion and Batian, and face for home. The rappel was excruciatingly slow because of the altitude, the bitter alpine weather, the weight of the wet icy ropes, and the heavy pack. However, training and endurance seemed to be working. We were making solid progress and each pitch took us closer to terra firma two thousand feet below. Then it happened.

I knew intuitively that I was making a mistake but I talked myself into carrying on anyway. The routine was the same every time. Check the belay. Check the ATC device (for friction) and the rope connection. Check the belay again. Unclip the safety sling. Tie it off to the harness on the left side—away from the rope feeding through the device. Step on to the edge and launch onto the descent pitch (roughly 150 feet each time. Given that the cliff was 2000 feet that meant there was at least 14 rappels to the surface below). The mistake began with a thought. We were about seven pitches from the summit. What could go wrong if I tie the safety sling onto the right side instead of the left side of the harness? I was tired, my arms ached, I was hungry. What could go wrong? I stepped off and launched onto the springiness of the rope. It felt good. Suddenly, I found myself hanging upside down, my feet above my head rotating freely about twenty feet away from the face on a vertical stretch. The pack was dragging me down. Apparently, the sling had got caught up in the double ropes and was solidly engaged in the ATC—effectively stopping the ropes from feeding through any further. I was stuck. Upside down. Swinging and rotating 1500 feet above Africa... My own weight and the weight of the pack were exacerbating the jam making it impossible to release. My arms were so tired already that I could not even pull myself upright. I swung there in disbelief—alone. My intuitional voice had been right all along. Do not tie it off to the right! Don't change the pattern!

None of my teammates could hear or see me because the wind continued to howl and the snow was whipping like sharp razors at my face. It was hard not to look down upside down at the revolving floor way below. If this wasn't the end, and maybe it was, then there had to be a solution. I quickly abandoned the idea of jettisoning the pack because I would need the contents if I survived. We were still two maybe three days away from civilization. I regretted immediately not having prussik loops attached and at the ready. They were carefully coiled in the pack. That was another mistake. Altitude, cold, hunger, sleep deprivation and fatigue. Still I should have known better. I needed a miracle. Then I noticed it. Twenty feet away, a good pendulum swing, attached to the face of the wall, was a karabiner and sling. It was white. About two inches, I surmised. What were the odds?

Slowly, I began to imitate like the pendulum in my grandfather's clock, back and forth above Africa, getting closer to and then, exasperatingly farther from, the spot on the face where the white sling dazzled my upside-down dim vision. Questions ached in my brain. Maybe it was old and not safe? I reached out and almost grabbed it. I swung away thirty feet again. Next time I crashed into the face, but well to the left of it. Ten more pendules... I was gaining in angle towards it. Finally, I had it firmly in my grasp. I grabbed on for dear life. It held. I tied on, and felt the safety line go taut around my middle. I was happy to once more face the world upright again. *Mirabile dictu*[11] I mumbled a prayer of thanks to the anonymous party who had abandoned this lifesaving sling and piton. But more so I was grateful for the immaculate positioning of my mistake and this rescue device. A few feet higher or lower and it would be impossible to reach. I felt safe tied on to this piton eerie on the face of nowhere.

This time I didn't trust my inner voice. I tested every thought twice. Undo ATC... Release rope. Do not let it go. How to hold on to it? Need both hands... don't remove gloves. Too cold... Mouth. Hold the rope with teeth. Ice bite. Breathe. Build the entire system from scratch. Harness, slings, ropes, device. Finally, it was done. Wait. Do it all over again. Don't trust the voice yet. Harness, slings, ropes, device... Right.

Then it dawned on me. I was going to have to let go. Let go... swing wildly out over the void again. But I just got away from that, just got tied up and safe. But there it was. I had to let go of my safe eerie of I was to get off the rope and let the others descend after me. They were completely unaware of my predicament or what I had just accomplished. One last time I checked the device, knots, ropes, and harness. My hand rested automatically on the karabiner screw to release the safety sling. I rechecked the device, the knots, the ropes, the harness... and it was over. I let go!

As I swung out over Africa once more I knew that my life was changed forever. The cold air that bit into my nose and eyes, only served to remind me how grateful I was to be alive... to be experiencing the now. The transformation that I had sought months earlier was upon me. The rope inched smoothly through the ATC. I was descending down... down... down, great big leaps with redefined energy and in a few minutes I was firm on a narrow ledge. I tied on. The safety sling was now my dearest ally. Tugging gingerly on the ropes I was anxious to let my teammates above know I was off the rope and belayed. I was relieved to feel the answering tug relayed back through the stiff and frozen but very real lifeline. They were safe too. Automatically, I turned my thoughts to setting up the next pitch down in expectation of their imminent arrival. I told no one about the incident until we were lunching in Nairobi a week later. The enduring lesson for me was about my intuitive inner voice and letting go.

Why don't we readily let go? Could it be fear? Fear of the unknown is a common issue for people who are, undoubtedly, questioning their faith in the final hours. Our attachment to physical things is the same attachment we have to our physical bodies. If we learned to live more simply, not afraid to let go of the clutter that we insist has value in our lives, we would be much more willing to also let go of the physical body.

One's faith should be a deep 'knowing' that we are going to God when all is said and done. Years of conditioning and self-judgment, however, causes even the most devout to question. The process of passing from this world is, of course, each person's experience. It must be examined on all levels.

My husband has diabetes and has also been diagnosed with cancer. He refuses to manage his sugar and eats a poor diet despite my constant protest. How can I best help him without driving myself crazy?

First, you must see this as his journey and karmically what he needs to work out at this time. Yes it is terrible he is not managing his food. I will go back to the beginning of this book and the four learning modes that were mentioned. Find out what his primary learning function is and approach him from that place. If he is visual you need to get him on the computer and have him read about diabetes and diet. If he is tonal have his doctor talk to him about food choices and monitoring his sugar. If he is kinesthetic introduce him to other diabetics and let him feel what they are going through. If he is mental then give him the facts in books and on tape! Medical journals would be the best solution for that particular learning mode. Then take yourself out of the equation. You can only take care of yourself so you are healthy and able to care for him. Give him your boundaries and let him know what his options are. If someone isn't fully cooperating in the marriage to help the other person with their illness then usually that is a good sign the inner child is at the helm. What can you do about this? Suggest they see a therapist and get some emotional bodywork done. If they are not interested in that approach and would rather self-destruct then you must take care of yourself and realize you have only so much energy and time in the day. Let him know you are willing to fix the right foods and if he doesn't want to eat them he can cook for himself. Let him know if he continues to self-destruct you will be forced to admit him to a care facility if he should go into a diabetic coma. There are consequences to our actions and without considering our loved ones in the process it becomes a much more difficult path. When we act from a place of selfishness or self-centered thinking we forget that others around us are the ones who ultimately will be taking care of us when we are ill or bedridden. Realizing this ahead of time is like having life insurance in that you want to treat those around you with love and kindness for it is those very people who will be caring for you when you might least expect it. If there are issues between you that haven't been resolved then I suggest you experience therapy for your emotional body so you can keep yourself balanced and strong.

There is a solution. If people are irritating you or causing you to feel something other than joy, you must go inside of yourself and find where you could possibly have that behavior yourself. Maybe it manifests in a different way with you and it takes a great deal of honesty with oneself to get to this place of healing. A great example is the last question where the woman didn't know how to get her husband who is ill to eat right and take care of himself through his illness. There is a way to heal that. She must go inside of herself and find where she can be obstinate or want to push up against authority and love that part of herself and more importantly forgive that part of her.

It can be difficult to identify the feeling in the emotional body as we all have the story and our part in that story. But often times when we are in the role we don't see the forest through the trees. The anger and upset that a loved one isn't taking care of themselves and leaving that burden ultimately up to their spouse is not leaving any room for the spouse to process but more or less be on high alert at all times. That level of fight or flight can be exhausting and can burn out the caregiver before the partner who is ill or dying.

THE MENTAL BODY

The Mental body is our rational side and the ever-present thought process we rely on. In the death experience our mind is usually out of the way. It is the mind that has all of the reasoning and cross-examination as to why we should not be in this predicament at this time. And like good lawyers we stand and defend ourselves and explain to the judge why he should let us go free. The mind also insists upon replaying the past. We relive many memories, as we are moving towards departure. Our parents come to mind. Many stories about our childhood and ourselves flow out of us like a vast river. Some are encumbered by mental illness or dementia and through this process relive the past and rework how we executed our life during stress-filled times. The following story is a personal story about my grandfather that serves to illustrate the difficulty (but also the incredible insights) that accompany the dying process when the elderly loved one is quite sick.

When I was a young adult, my Norwegian grandfather was in the hospital suffering from Alzheimer's. I went to visit him and he recognized me.

"Sonja, I'm so glad you came." My grandfather was in this overstuffed chair, sitting in this big hallway, and you could see the light coming through the windows. They were making beautiful patterns of light across the floor. He was by himself and I went and sat with him in the chair.

"You know grandpa, I'm really happy to be here with you." He patted my hand and said he was glad I came to see him. Then we just sat in silence together. Inside of my mind and heart I asked archangel Gabriel to come and help my grandfather. Suddenly, Gabriel appeared at the end of the hallway. Abruptly my grandfather looked over at me.

"Sonja, there's a Big angel at the end of the hallway."

"You can see that?" I was surprised.

"Yeah I can see that!" His voice relayed a quizzical ambiguity. "What's he doing here?"

"Well he came to help you."

My grandfather just smiled, sat back in his chair. "Oh, that's nice!"

This is a great example of the mental body being altered through Alzheimer's and my grandfather being able to experience the spiritual body right away. He lost his mother when he was very young, a life event that left him impoverished in some aspects all throughout his life afterwards. This is how I experienced his illness. My interpretation of his disease was simple; it allowed him revert back into an infant state to get the love and nurturing (from caregivers at the convalescent home) that he so longed for when he was a baby.

The family however experienced a proud successful man losing his ability to reason and care for himself. They agonized over his descent and felt he was no longer the man they had known. This lack of understanding corresponds to the human experience of shallow vision; not understanding what we worldly beings must process and work through in order to depart this world and move into the next realm.

The Mental Body is complex because of a lifetime of conditioning and pattern memorization. We respond to our thought process faster than we realize and the mental body is often stimulated by the emotional body. When making the journey home many people believe there are signs and markers to look for as we cross over. This is true in that our relatives and loved ones are waiting for us; to help and guide us as we make the journey to the other side.

THE EMOTIONAL BODY

The **Emotional Body** is the hardest to separate from because it is made of the fibers that attach us to the physical body. It is the part of us that feels sadness, pain and sorrow at our life's end. But the emotional body is also the part of us that can turn the experience around; to feel joy that we are being released and that we will feel better soon!

The quality of your passage is up to you

The process of crossing over is the marker for your life; how you exit, and how you re-enter the next time. We have many feelings for people, places, and events from our lives that are karmically connected. The threads of our history are entwined with events from this lifetime. For instance, we experience a good feeling when visiting Rome, but we feel scared when we get into a boat to cross the ocean. These are the kinds of karmic memories that we carry in our souls.

Lifetime through lifetime such karma endures through events that are neither settled nor forgiven. We bring that pain, experience, or memory into the next lifetime. In my experience the idea that we bring karmic memories with us (when we are born into this world) can be a difficult concept for people to grasp. So how does it really work? The following story illustrates how an illness or pain in this world had its origins in another place and time.

A client experienced chronic neck pain year after year. After MRI's and cat scans doctors were at a loss to know what to tell her. Their investigations found absolutely nothing to report that could be connected to the pain. She was frustrated and desperate. She called me believing I was a last hope.

I began holistically by looking for larger patterns. Through a past-life reading I was able to discover several related calamities. She had been beheaded in a past lifetime around 1200 A.D. At that time, she could not fathom being beheaded, nor did she die with a peaceful thought of losing her head! She was shocked and unable to comprehend the moment.

When she incarnates again she manifests exactly that same event to try to heal what had happened before. She is beheaded again. She dies this time too with shocking disbelief that this could happen to her. This client experiences three more lifetimes where she ends up being hung.

I went back and cleared the karma of these lives. She experienced immediate relief, and has had no neck pain to this day. Her shock and disbelief is what carried that karma through each life, holding her captive to suffering and pain.

As we experience the emotional body we have an assortment of feelings that come to the surface. Fear is usually the most pronounced. My father's story is the culmination of fear and release that combined the mental and emotional bodies into the spiritual body.

On Christmas day, 2007, my father was taken to the hospital. The diagnosis was a perforated bowel that was inoperable. He had suffered a stroke eight years prior, and had lost all feeling in the left side of his body. This put him in a wheelchair. My father was a contractor and world traveler. He was bright, positive and enthusiastic about life. The story line comes from another place and time. For Harry to experience a major stroke and to end up in a wheelchair was shocking, to say the least. He was also someone who suffered from being a socially acceptable alcoholic, meaning he drank after work, but he drank heavily. This meant that when he had his stroke, because he had so much alcohol in his system, he was unable to go on Coumadin right away to thin his blood. They had to wait for him to detox. I had the privilege of going through dad's detox from alcohol as I sat in the hospital for a week after his stroke. We talked about the dog that was in the room, and we talked about the hand. He always had this vision that there was a hand in the bed, or somewhere near him. When I would see Grandma, his mother, standing there in spirit form I would talk to him about it.

"Dad, do you see Grandma?"

He would respond, "Yeah, do you?"

So he figured out at that time that I was able to see what he saw. That clairvoyant side of me was new to my dad as he had never really prescribed to a spiritual life. He was raised Presbyterian, very strict and a definite heaven and hell belief system. He was never really exposed or had any spiritual feelings. In fact, at one time I remember him saying, "we live, we die, and then we're put in the ground. That's it." And that's pretty much how he lived his life, like "this is it, this is his life, and when he's done he'll be six feet under and that would be it." Eventually he went into the VA home, and spent the remaining years of his life there. He had a fun version of dementia, in that he believed that mom lived in the popcorn machine at the end of the hall, and that he was still flying fighter jets! He had served in the Korean War and believed he was still there. He was also building houses and often talked to us about the plans and the architect. Eight years later, this past Christmas, we ended up taking him to the hospital because he had a really high fever. It turned out that he had a perforated bowel that was inoperable because his condition was so weak. He'd already had a pacemaker put in when he had the stroke and he was certainly not going to make it through a major surgery. The doctor told us that all we could do was make him comfortable, and when the pain level got to be at a certain place we would start him on morphine. The doctor also told us it would just be a matter of time. Over the course of the next four days he went through a tremendous process. The first part of the journey he remained relatively clear and was able to talk with me in a way I had not heard from him in years. At one point he said to me.

"I'm not sure of where I'm going."

"Well Dad, actually you're going to God, no question about it"

"Well I don't know, I don't think so." He seemed lost. So we took a break and I went back to my mom's house to shower and get cleaned up. I tuned in to my dad, and sure enough it was his first day of receiving morphine, and I could see lower astral plane entities around his bed. I knew immediately what it was. I knew that it was dad's manifestation from his fear. So I cleared all of it and I went to the hospital and said to him "it's gone."

He looked at me and his voice was quiet. "Did you see him? Did you see him? Satan was here, and I saw him."

"Yeah Dad, and he's gone. Do you see him now?"

"No."

"Well I cleared him, he's gone."

He looked at me and he had big tears in his eyes. "Do you promise?"

"Yes, I promise! He's gone! Never to come back!" He just squeezed my hand tight.

As a child I had placed my father on a high pedestal. I thought that he was the strongest, brightest man alive. But now dad was scared. He was really afraid of what would happen after his death. I was grateful I had the gifts to help him go through this major passage. He had so much fear about going to hell it made me wonder what kinds of things happened to him in Korea and what pain he suffered from the war. I talked to him and I reassured him.

"Dad, you're not going to hell, that's just not possible." My mother, sisters, and I asked the local priest, even though we were not Catholic, to come in and talk to dad. The priest was a great man, who takes care of the police department and the fire department, and everyone in town. He told my dad he was a wonderful man and that God was waiting for him. He had a great conversation with him about where he was going, completely backing up what I had been saying and then he said a prayer over him. After four days everyone, including the staff is tired and spent. We've all been sleeping in his room with him. At this point he's not able to take in any water, in fact he will not allow an IV to be put into him. He's also not able to eat because of his perforated bowel, and the doctors are afraid he's going to go septic. My sister Karolyn was sitting on the bed with her back against the wall. My father was in his bed across the room, and mom was standing right over him, holding his hand. She turned—I was sitting right behind her—looked at me, and said, "Sonja, Sonja, I think this is it!" I ran to dad and stood by my mom. She immediately buried her head in my shoulder, sobbing. I took dad's hand and on the third exhale, I watched him take his last breath.

I spoke out loud, "okay dad, this is it. You can do it. I know you can do it! It's time to go to the light."

I watched my father lift up out of his body, and he stood on the other side of the bed. He looked at me, his eyes got really big and really bright, and he said, "I did it!"

"Yes, dad, you did it. I am so proud of you!"

He didn't realize that he could walk, because he had been in a wheelchair for eight years. He just didn't realize he could walk without a body! He was so proud of himself.

"Dad you have to go to the light now."

"Why? Why now?"

"Because now's the time." I could see it. Right behind him was this huge, bright light, and this big hallway. My uncle Lloyd, dad's brother who passed away a year before, was standing there. I heard his voice.

"Come on Harry!" He put his arm around my dad and he smiled at me.

"It's okay dad, you can go now, go to the light." I watched them both walk down what looked like a long hallway. My relatives were dispersed through this great cosmic tunnel. I saw my uncles and aunts and grandparents. They were all there. And dad was walking towards the light. I followed him as far as I could. It got really bright towards the end, and something pulled me back. I felt it was my own guides keeping me here. My father made it to the light, and it was the most beautiful event I had ever experienced. I was so happy, and I was just standing there by his body applauding while my mother was sobbing deep into my shoulder.

I woke up really early in the morning. I was in that half-dream, half-awake state. My dad was standing next to the bed. He looked at me and spoke. "Honey, I just came back to tell you how grateful I am for what you did for me. You really are my angel." He put his hands on my head, and I felt him. I felt him touch me. It was like my whole head was encompassed in gold light. He had the biggest smile on his face.

"I just can't thank you enough, you really helped me."

"Be sure and go through your healing time and then come back and see me." I was so happy to see him.

Since then, he has come to see me many times. He usually comes when something's going on with my mom. He tells me to call her, or make sure I check on her. My father is now walking, totally recovered from his stroke. He has an amazing appearance—youthful like he was in his mid to late 40's. It was a beautiful passing and something that completely changed my life.

DO WE REALLY NEED TO BE AFRAID? NO.

IS IT A TRANSITION THAT WE MAKE DIFFICULT FOR OUR-SELVES BECAUSE OF OUR FEAR? YES.

IF WE LET GO OF OUR FEAR WOULD IT BE A LOT EASIER? YES.

The emotional body delivers our experiences on a feeling level. In the example of my father above, it was obvious that he had a logjam of emotions that came out at the end; with tears. He knew he would be traveling alone on that journey ahead. But the emotional body is simply processing the feeling.

This is exactly what we are supposed to do while in physical form. We feel sadness and pain with the departure, but there can also be joy. This is experienced when we realize that we are about to be reunited with our loved ones and our pets that have crossed over.

It is my understanding from the spirit realm that we have a responsibility to the soul group that we came through. Consequently, when we pass we do not incarnate right away. We look after the children and grandchildren in our families. In effect we become guardian angels to those left behind.

From a feeling standpoint, it is well understood that children feel their guardian angels around them and often will identify Grandma or Grandpa without ever having known them. The feeling of pain and discomfort that accompanies the dying process, relates to a history of not feeling our feelings until, suddenly at the end (and while in review of one's life), the emotional body spills all demanding we deal with them.

Part of the process that accompanies the task of feeling one's feelings is forgiveness. This one singular act can release more karma than anything else we could attempt. It is a requirement for being in human form, but very often the last thing anyone chooses to do. When feeling our feelings and discovering we have unsettled business, we need to allow ourselves to forgive that person, place, or thing. Then we have to let it go. Once we release these unresolved feelings we create a first class ticket for our journey! There can be lots of joy because we did our work in the emotional body while here on Earth.

~~

GRIEF

The grieving process is a complex journey—and not to be ignored. There are many stages to go through. It is important to remember that when we do not allow ourselves time and space to grieve properly we set up patterns that force us to deal with grief in the future.

Grief comes in many forms such as the loss of a relationship, job, home, empire, loved one, or pet. When we are taught as children not to feel bad (because maybe the family dog 'Spot' just died) we are learning to put our feelings on the shelf; to replace the loss with another pet. In this way we are trained to feel 'good' again before we have fully processed our pain and grief. It is easy to see how that might negatively impact someone throughout his/her life here on earth.

Society also forces us to build patterns in our lives that lead to grief. Events outside our control (wars, systems failing, or changing economies) often create large circles of fear and loss of trust. When we experience grief we have a reduced ability to concentrate. We often feel we are losing our minds and are unable to concentrate on anything. Social norms and well-meaning loved ones often minimize our pain and suffering with a good story about someone else who has lost more or suffered more.

WHEN WE COMPARE WE MINIMIZE

WHEN WE MINIMIZE WE LOSE THE OPPORTUNITY TO PROCESS AND FEEL OUR FEELINGS.

FEELING OUR FEELINGS IS THE MAIN WORK WE ARE HERE TO DO ON EARTH.

THE SPIRITUAL BODY

The spiritual body is the part of us that is connected to God or the Universe. We have what is called a soul and this is the very essence of the spiritual body. We bring karma with us lifetime to lifetime—comprising unresolved issues such as a specific death experience, lost love, abandonment, betrayal, or abuse. From that respect, attention to karma is important.

KARMA

We have sat on both the receiving and delivering sides of karma and yet we wonder; 'why does this happen to me.' Why do I have this 'bad luck' or why didn't I ever find my 'true love' in this lifetime? These are common questions that seem to come up time and again with clients I counsel. Here's the problem. Sure there is karma. We all have karma. But if we do not go back to review our past lives, we do not have the information to clear this karma. The karmic history with which we travel is immense and can be the key to unraveling the many mysteries in our lives. In this way we can heal.

The spiritual body holds the energy for our life force. As we prepare to depart our physical body that life forces becomes quite visible; it starts to move up the legs. As we leave the body we literally see the energy leave the physical body—the legs and torso turn blue. The soul exits out the top of the head and has an immediate connection with what is called the light. The light is a large tunnel or hallway that is the passageway to the spirit realm. Many people are aware of a bright light at the end of a tunnel. This bright light at the end of this tunnel is where you will be headed. All of your relatives and loved ones will be there to help you.

SUDDEN DEATH

This journey is a process that can be missed if someone dies suddenly. It happened without warning and they are confused as to where they are, i.e. what state they are in. I have helped only a handful of people like this. They were trying to go to the light after they had died but didn't know what had happened to them due to the sudden death experience. Most of the time they are trying to communicate with their loved ones, still obsessed with completing what they felt they needed to complete. This, in itself, is another good reason to end each day with everything said and done; all actions taken and all wrongs forgiven!

This experience (not going to the light due to confusion after a sudden death) is something that each soul has to come to terms with much in the same way Patrick Swayze had to help his girlfriend in the movie 'Ghost' before he could go on to the light. Some souls get stuck and need the help of someone who is clairvoyant; someone in effect, who can see them and assist them. In my experience this is not a common occurrence. The spirit body is a catchall and often needs to be cleared before passing, so that we are leaving with one bag instead of five. In other words, the energy we have in our soul (and all of the experiences throughout our current and past lives) comes with us. For this reason, it is important for people to realize who they have been and to embody that energy so that they can bring all parts of themselves into the current life.

When we leave this life it is equally important to have peace and forgiveness for any and all parts we might have struggled with. Clients often ask me, "But how do we know all of these parts of ourselves? Truly, it is not easy, but we must be open to knowing. The spiritual body gives us signs all of the time, showing us who we are connected to karmically. Think about your life today. We meet people we feel we have known. We travel to places we feel we have been to before. We have dreams about places we have never been to, or about people we have never met. This is the spirit body giving us signs of who we have been and who we are karmically connected to.

SOUL MATE

One of the most common questions that people ask me is, "Who is my soul mate?" The answer is simple. We have not just one but many soul mates. To single out one person seems impossible through all of the lives we have lived with people, and through relationships we have experienced. The ones we have karma with, the ones we tend to feel connected to, are the very people we were in relationships with in our last lifetime or several lifetimes ago. Sometimes we spend many lifetimes with a person trying to resolve and heal the events that have occurred (again and again).

FAMILY

Do we come through the same family each time? We each evolve at different rates. Our consciousness is what we are working on while incarnate in an earthly body. The goal is to bring a higher consciousness into our physical experience. Our connections to our family members are strong. Karmically speaking, they form many attachments between us.

There is a good chance you will manifest with your family members again, but with different roles. You may incarnate as the mother this time; your mom is your daughter. Meanwhile, your father is your brother and your brother is your child. We change family pods as well. Vibrationally and karmically, we are matching ourselves up with the best lessons to be learned and to heal by.

AGING

The universe is extremely complex. Alignment for each soul (depending on what we have to learn karmically) is where we manifest into physical form. The journey out of this life and into the spirit realm involves a healing process. The spirit body carries the pain and suffering our physical body has endured. We get to heal on the other side and usually in that process people get younger in appearance. We tend to go back to a time in our physical life where we felt the best. My father looks around forty years old today, when I see him in the spirit realm. He was seventy-seven years old when he died.

Many people who ask me to reunite them with a loved one are surprised to find that their Aunt Mabel has a youthful appearance, resembling her age around 30. Some people are very happy when they pass and I see them looking just about the age they were when they left. Most people, however, spend a great deal of time reminiscing over a time in their lives—a chance they missed, a job they might have taken, a girl they might have married, a man they might have left, or a child they might have kept. There are so many stories that stay with the spirit body that become the intense creation of karma. This is why forgiveness is so important in our experience here on earth.

ALIGNMENT OF THE FOUR BODIES
The quality of your passage is up to you. What does that really mean? How you choose to look at an event or experience in your life is up to you. You can filter it through some victim pattern that you learned from your parents, who learned it from their parents... and on and on. At the same time, you can take responsibility for your experience and see what you are supposed to learn from an event. How is the universe (your God) talking to you through any given situation? Do we have

the courage to face our shortcomings; to forgive ourselves in order to be able to take it one step further and forgive those who we perceived have wronged us?

What is our perception that someone has wronged us, if we do not have the full story of what exists between each of us karmically? If we do not have access to that information then the high road would be to forgive that person for any pain or wrongdoing they might have caused you from the time of creation until now. And of course you would ask that they forgive you for any pain or wrongdoing you might have caused them from the time of creation until now. These processes are stored in our mental body. They are experienced in the emotional and physical bodies and ultimately clear the spiritual body. This is a different way of looking at life. It is the alignment we desire to make our passage with joy.

QUESTIONS AND ANSWERS

What if my loved one is terminally ill and I am their caregiver and unable to do anything but watch them suffer and feel bad?

First, look at their pain and suffering as theirs. You do not have the same karma as your loved one. They have lived many lives and have accumulated karma that is allowing them this experience. View it as their opportunity to learn about illness, suffering, pain and eventually, releasing the body. You are with them and thus a vibrational match. So there is something for you to learn in this situation as well.

But they didn't ask for this to happen. This is tragic. They are suffering horribly from this illness. How could this possibly be teaching them anything?

Yes, they are suffering and it is tragic. However, they have issues in the emotional body that need to be addressed. Most illnesses begin in the emotional body. The sooner we address such issues the more we have a chance of working through our pain. There is a great possibility that past lives are a clue into this illness. It is likely that they have suffered and died from illness in many lifetimes.

From this perspective, they are re-creating this pattern again so they might evolve in their experience.

I feel guilty because my husband is ill and in a home and I am left not knowing what to do. I want to have a life, and feel I am missing out on life due to his illness. I am feeling so guilty I don't know what to do.

This guilty feeling is very common for people in your situation. Yet the realization that we must complete what we came here to do is very important. What does that mean? Why are we here?

We are here to love at the deepest level of our beings.

Granted, some people find comfort sitting with their loved one and caring for them. At the same time, others experience the need to live and not feel their own life-force is leaving because it is wrapped up in this person that is ill.

Forgiveness helps in this situation. We must forgive ourselves first for our feelings. Next we must forgive them for being ill. This act of forgiveness will release us from the shame and guilt that is self-inflicted by the inner judge. Once we have released ourselves from this place (a place of I should or I could have) we can then approach our lives from the perspective of living. Start with your everyday environment. Have I recycled everything I could? Have I cleaned out the closet and kept only what I need?

Forgiveness applies also to our personal relationships. Sometimes they are going through their own transformations. Have you forgiven them for any transgressions and, vice versa, have they offered forgiveness to you? Have you told them that you love them from the deepest level of your heart? When forgiveness releases you, the mere act of living your life is taking care of you. No one else is going to do that for you. You can only take care of you! If you take on someone else's pain you not only rob them of their own experience, but you cause them to miss the opportunity to grow.

But if I don't stay in control my partner doesn't eat right or take care of himself the way the doctors have told him to do so. I am afraid he will have a much bigger calamity and I will be stuck with being the nursemaid.

Boundaries are key in this case and must be applied across the board no matter what your situation is. People will pull at your energy, especially if they are dying. They are probably frightened and extremely unsure about making that journey alone.

How do you create healthy boundaries? You recognize what is your stuff and what is their stuff. You are not ill. You need to eat right, take your vitamins and stay healthy! If they choose to not eat right and there is a potential disaster pending you need to give them boundaries and lay it out for them. Say something like this:

"You take care of yourself and eat right. We have more time together and we are strong for each other. You don't eat right. Your body gives out and you end up in the emergency room in a coma. Here is the name of the home we will be moving you to once you have stabilized."

There is no room for protest, as everyone's insurance will dictate what can or cannot be done in the extreme. But, to victimize yourself by feeling this person is not taking care of himself— thus sabotaging your life—is an old approach! It's time for a new approach. The need to be in control is your own fear. If we trust God or the Universe has our back we will be fine with whatever comes our way.

To examine this further we must look at the emotional body one more time. We all carry emotional wounding from childhood, no matter what kind of family environment we grew up in. This is often the key to uncovering where we stopped developing at an emotional level. When our loved one is sick and facing that journey to the spirit realm he or she will often experience their inner child. The inner child is with us our whole lives and it is up to us to parent this child once we become adults.

The inner child is the part of us that is playful and carefree. Many of us don't realize that part of us that was wounded is actually in charge and running the show. If you grew up with any kind of dysfunction in your family, your little adult is used to stepping-up and taking charge. We, as adults, must take responsibility for this inner child. We must nurture, parent, and love him/her so that we can heal the pain and avoid emotional triggers that keep us from forgiveness and inner peace.

To equate all of this to the passage of death we must have an understanding of what is still unresolved internally. We need to know how to address this while we are preparing for our journey to the spirit realm.

The key to understanding the inner child is to connect with the emotional body; to visualize the inner child walking up to you. Allow them to be whatever age is best for that moment. Ask the child how they are feeling. Then ask the child what they need from you at this time. Allow yourself to hear them with your eyes closed and listen with your stomach (kinesthetic modality). Pick that child up in your mind's eye and put them on your lap. Hug them; tell them you love them. Remind them that you are parenting them now and you will always protect them. Even when it is time to make the journey you will be in charge and keep them safe. Give the love and comfort to that inner child that you would want from others while you go through this difficult time. Tell the child you will honor their feelings. Do what you can to express their pain by visualizing your parents (or with whomever you might have experienced the emotional wounding). Go back to that time in your mind with your eyes closed and you inner child safe on your lap.

As you hold this child on your lap you are creating a safe place for the child. Allow the child to voice to whomever how he or she feels. Imagine the person to whom the child is expressing feelings as sitting across from you both. Get all of it out and let the child explain that he or she is just a child who doesn't want to carry this pain anymore. Then see the child reach inside of you and take out that pain—like a big balloon or giant blob and place it in a box right in front of your feet. Together, both you and the child, hand the box back to the people (or person) that wounded the child. Tell them you don't want to carry this anymore. Remind them that it was never yours to carry in the first place. Then have the child tell the person that he or she forgives them and that you also forgive them for any pain or wrongdoing they may have caused from the time of creation until now. Release them. See them walk away with the box in hand. This will allow you to release the emotional pain. Since emotional pain is connected to physical pain, it will also release from the physical body. Notice where you feel a release in the body!

Your mental body is very much involved in this process as it is allowing you to visualize these people and your inner child and your emotional body is processing all of it. The physical body releases it and the spiritual body heals from it.

How can I let my mother go, she is my world and we are so close?

You must realize you are close because you are karmically connected and you have a connection with her that goes throughout your lifetimes of being connected. Rest assured you will see her again as she will be waiting for you when it is your time to cross over. She will become a guardian angel to her grandchildren and find she has a lot to do in the spirit realm.

The spirit realm has many functions and is constantly keeping balance with the physical realm. The souls in the spirit realm are working hard to help us here in the physical realm. They have jobs in that they look after their family and loved ones. They attend school if they need extra review for their actions here on earth. They do not incarnate right away, unless it is a baby or small child who needs to come back and complete what was started. Families are karmic pods. We have a responsibility to the pod to take care of and bring along everyone in consciousness so that we can all evolve. Sometimes the family will not incarnate as a soul group until the whole family is in the spirit realm.

How long do we spend in the spirit realm until we incarnate again?

How we measure time on Earth is not the same in the spirit realm. Usually, I see a turn-around time between ten and thirty years.

My brother who is a veteran of war could not take the pain anymore so he committed suicide. Where did he go and what happened to his soul?

There are many people in your brother's situation, who cannot deal with their pain. This is the choice they make. What they find when they get to the other side is that they still have to deal with their pain. It doesn't go away. They no longer have the ability to communicate with and directly deal with people here on Earth. That is why so many souls contact me seeking to tell their families that they are sorry and begging for forgiveness.

Your brother is with God. He went to the light as all souls do. There is time for him to review his life; to learn in the spirit realm about the choice that he made and what that means for him karmically. He will have time to heal during this time of reviewing. The soul often stays with family and incarnates when the family pod is ready. Sometimes I see souls incarnate right away if they did not finish something here on Earth. Only God and that soul could know or understand this matter. Each person is unique. The soul's journey is extremely complex.

My daughter speaks ill of her father who passed away two years ago and I don't know how to help her to heal her feelings. What can she do to get through this so she isn't so angry towards him?

Post death pain and grievances do not go away unless we do the work. Your daughter needs processing work with her inner child, so that she can forgive him for any pain or wrongdoing he has caused her from the time of creation until now. Most people who have not forgiven a parent, for things that happened in the past, will carry that grief and actually hold that parent's spirit hostage, preventing them from making progress in the spirit realm. These spirits often come to me requesting I talk to a family member to set it right. From my perspective, the process of forgiveness is probably the most important and critical part of being human.

My brother died suddenly in a motorcycle accident and my family has not gotten over the loss. We cannot understand why God would take him from us when he was so young and vibrant. Please help us to understand this.

Your brother was taken from the earth suddenly due to his need to be on the other side to help in the spirit realm. He has as much a job over there as he did here on earth. The fact that he was called over early simply means that he has some history or karma that involves sudden death and he is still trying to work that out. He also has a need to care for his family in a different way. The spirit realm often tells me about their need to look after certain family members—to give them extra help from the other side. This is not a bad thing. We are able to know that our loved one didn't abandon us, but, rather, went over to the other side to help us. We must understand that both realms work hand-in-hand, maintaining a delicate balance between the two worlds. This is similar to how our earth is—in balance with humanity and the cosmos. It is all a state of delicate but perfect balance.

My husband has diabetes and has also been diagnosed with cancer. He refuses to manage his sugar and eats a poor diet despite my constant protests. How can I best help him without driving myself crazy?

Step back. You must see that this is your husband's journey. Understand what karma he needs to work out at this time. Yes, it is terrible he is not managing his food. Recall from earlier in this book where we discussed four learning modes. Knowing his preferred learning mode would help. Find out what his primary learning method is and approach him from that place. If he is visual, get him on a computer. Have him read about diabetes and diet. If he is tonal, have his doctor talk to him about food choices focusing in particular about monitoring his sugar intake. If he is kinesthetic, introduce him to other diabetics. Let him feel what they are going through. If he is mental, give him the straight facts in books or tapes. Medical journals would be a good solution for that particular learning style.

Then take yourself out of the equation. Remember, you can only take care of yourself. This way you stay healthy and are able to care for yourself and for him. Give him your boundaries. Let him know clearly what his options are. If someone isn't fully cooperating in a marriage (especially when it comes to illness) then usually that is a good sign that the inner child is at the helm. What can you do about this?

Suggest they see a therapist and get some emotional bodywork done. If they are not interested in that approach—would rather self-destruct, then you must take care of you. Please realize you have only so much energy and time in the day. Let your husband know you are willing to fix the right foods and if he doesn't want to eat them... he can cook for himself. Let him know that if he continues to self-destruct you will be forced to admit him to a care facility if he should go into a diabetic coma.

There are consequences to our actions and without considering our loved ones in the process it becomes a much more difficult path. When we act from a place of selfishness or self-centered thinking it hurts. We forget that those closest to us are the ones who ultimately will be taking care of us when we are bedridden. Realizing this ahead of time is like having life insurance. Treat people close to you with love and kindness, for it is those very people who will be caring for you when you might least expect it. If there are issues between you and your husband that haven't been resolved, I suggest that you embrace therapy for your emotional body so you can keep yourself balanced and strong.

If a partner or loved one is irritating you and causing you to feel something other than joy, your ultimate goal is to go inside of yourself; to find where you could possibly have that behavior as well. Maybe it manifests in a different way with you and it takes a great deal of honesty with oneself to get to this place of healing.

For example, in the last question where the woman didn't know how to get her husband to eat right that wife needed to look inside her also. She must find where she can be obstinate, to want to push up against authority. Then she must love that part of herself and, more importantly, forgive that part of herself.

It can be difficult to identify the feeling in the emotional body. We are all in it. We all have a story about someone else and our part in that story also. But when we are in the role we are often blinded. We miss the beauty of the forest because we are diverted by an apparent ugliness of some of the trees. The anger and upset that a loved one isn't taking care of themselves, in effect leaving that burden ultimately up to their spouse, is not leaving any room for that spouse to process emotionally. That individual is more or less on 'high alert' at all times. That level of fight or flight can be exhausting. It will inevitably burn out the caregiver first.

How do we take care of ourselves while dealing with someone else's passage into the spirit realm?

We must keep ourselves strong through meditation, breathing and boundaries. If we do not take care of ourselves how will we be able to be there for another?

Schedule your time as if you were at the office. From 9.00 to 10.00 you are helping your partner. Let them rest from 10.00 to 11.00 while you meditate or do yoga. Take the time to get out for a walk. If you schedule them you will make the time to do these things. If you need someone there to cover for you while you are out then you must put him/her on the schedule as well. These are simple boundaries that allow you the time and energy to be there for your loved ones.

How do I find my own inner peace when my mother is dying and in so much pain?

Each soul has it's own journey. We can empathize with others but we must be careful not go into sympathy with them. There is a subtle but strict difference between empathy and sympathy. Know it. Empathy emanates from the heart. This is a natural state for us to experience love and support, and without taking on a loved one's pain. Sympathy is from the belly. It is translated in energy from the belly by going out to. It is rarely grounded. Many people are kinesthetic and would benefit from learning to ground their energy. This would allow them to feel what others might be feeling, but prevents their energy going out from the second chakra to take on their pain. A chakra is an energy center. Chakras are in the energy field and connect deep at the center of the body into a vertical power currant. There are seven main chakras on the front and back of the body.

We are familiar with painful stomach cramps in the abdomen as a direct result of a loved one being sick. We easily take on their pain. This is an example of our being in sympathy with the loved one.

We do it automatically. It is hard not to go there when a loved one is ill and/or dying. The best way to handle this energy is to stay grounded—grounding the energy from the second chakra.

What happens when people die and we are not ready for it? We experience long periods of grief?

Cathy came to me recently to have some closure with a dear friend she had lost years ago. Mary Anne was in the spirit realm and came to me almost as quickly as Cathy walked through the door. She cried tears of sadness; sadness, and joy, and everything in-between. She was deeply moved and awed to be in Mary Anne's presence again. Cathy told me that I had shared things with her that only Mary Anne and Cathy could know. Mary Anne was someone Cathy dearly loved. She had been taken suddenly and unexpectedly from this world at the tender age of eighteen. Mary Anne's death was a mirror image of Cathy's own brush with death a year earlier. For over a decade Cathy had desperately struggled with a complicated grief reaction.

Although, she felt she had turned a corner and was able to move forward after a decade of deep grief, she found solace through her reading with me. Mary Anne's loving presence helped her find the encouragement to forgive the drunk driver who had killed Mary Anne and her parents. For the first time, Cathy felt deep compassion and empathy for this man's suffering and a deeper realization that Mary Anne was/is always with her. From this place she could be at peace with herself. She attained a new level of understanding and was no longer stuck in her emotional body. She was able to process and clear all four essential bodies. Consequently, she felt relief in the physical, deep movement in the emotional, a new understanding in the mental, and transformation in the spiritual.

Who is there waiting for us when it is our time to go?

An elderly woman who was in hospital suffering from stage-three stomach cancer spoke to me. Her son had approached me seeking help.

"You know, I really think my mom would benefit from talking to you, and I just wondered if I could arrange an appointment for her to talk to you. She's in the hospital, but I feel like she's not settled on some of her emotional issues and she's going through this cancer. Please, can you talk to her?" I spoke with his mother on the phone, and I instantly started getting flashes of what happened to her as a child. She had been beaten severely by her father when she was young. We talked about it and she stayed very calm throughout our conversation. Her father and mother both came through to me. Her mother spoke first.

"Please forgive us." She implored.

Her father also wanted her forgiveness. The most beautiful exchange happened when her parents told her they were waiting for her when it was her time to go. She was incredibly happy to hear that and to know they were both there in the spirit realm waiting for her.

The most profound part of this was that I could see Mother Mary standing next to her bed. Her presence is ominous when she appears to me and there is a bright white light around her. Mary asked me to tell this woman that she could hear her prayers; that she was with her and would be with her always. She told me to tell her that she was going to help her, especially when it was her time to cross over.

The elderly woman started crying when I told her this. "I've been praying to the Virgin Mary every day, asking for her to help me."

It was such a beautiful confirmation to her that her prayers were being heard and answered. She knew that she was protected and had a lot of loved ones, including the Virgin Mary looking after her.

MIRACLES

Recently I was working-out in the gym (doing my mile on the treadmill). On the machine next to me was a gentleman walking energetically also. He looked to be in his late 50's. I was at the end of my run and had slowed to a walk. All the while my neighbor walked briskly beside me. Suddenly there was a cry.

"Oh no!" It was a gentleman behind both of us. Out of the corner of my eye I witnessed the man next to me going backward as if riding a conveyer belt. He had a blank look on his face. He dropped like a stone to his knees. Without thinking, I hit the clear button and jumped off my treadmill. I saw the side of his face hit the edge of his machine. I pulled his body off the still moving roller, onto the floor. He went into convulsions.

Turning him onto his side, I held his head while he convulsed again and again.

"Get help, call 911." I was shouting at the only person who saw what was happening.

I prayed to all the angels and my guides to help this man. I asked God to not take him yet. I saw my guides standing there as I called out to them with every ounce of spiritual voice that I had. I realized that he was having a heart attack. In a calm voice, I told him softly in his ear he would be ok.

"Don't worry. I am here." I said over and over. "Help is coming."

My trainer was downstairs working with a client and had heard the yelling at the top of the stairs. He came running. Several other people came. I continued to hold his head in my hands. Slowly I watched his soul leave his body. I could see his legs go pale. They began to turn a light shade of blue. As it moved up his body, his soul exiting out the top of his head. Another man who was an EMT came to our side. I reported that he had stopped breathing.

"He is having a heart attack." I heard my empty words.

He told me to roll him on his back. He started CPR. All the while I could see the man's soul. It was about three feet in the air floating above the body.

I told him that I had asked the angels to come and help him, and that he was needed here on earth. I then watched him slip back into his body. Suddenly, he gasped for air. His eyes shot open. The paramedics had arrived. They were busily applying devices to his body. They attached a defibrillator.

I had moved to the wall where I held vigil with my guides. There was a roar of sound in my ears. I could only hear the spirit realm as if I was under water. They carried him downstairs after he regained consciousness. As I passed by the gurney

I told him he would be just fine. In fact, he is still just fine today after a brief stay at the hospital.

He suffered what is known as a sudden heart attack, of which the recovery rate is close to none. He states he remembers nothing. I felt as if I held his soul for a time—the time it took for him to have the heart attack and assess what was happening. He decided to come back into his body and regain consciousness.

With an experience such as this I can only attest to the fact that we all cross over. There is a place to go to that is beautiful and all-enveloping with love. When I talk to the spirit realm they tell me they are in a profound state of love. It is difficult to find words to describe it. Senses help, but only just. I have smelled fragrances that are so beautiful, nothing compares. The feeling I have experienced when angels come into a room is beyond description. The all-enveloping love from God and the Universe fills space so profoundly it moves the spirit. Unworldly is a meager and pitiably inadequate description of the feeling.

FORGIVENESS

By now you must be fully aware that forgiveness is central to the ideas of this book. It is the beginning and the end of living.

The death process is not fully understood and completed without the process of forgiveness. Forgiveness is the key ingredient to a successful passage into the spirit realm. We have lifetimes of experience in making this passage to and from the earth. With the element of forgiveness we have the opportunity to clear our karma and raise our consciousness. Each time we do this we are helping humanity raise consciousness and we are evolving in our incarnations that eventually bring us full circle and enlightenment.

Getting to this place requires work on all four levels of the essential bodies.

WHY IT IS SO DIFFICULT FOR PEOPLE TO FORGIVE

The process of forgiveness is often easier said than done. Most people struggle with forgiveness—not necessarily the concept of forgiveness but the actual practice of forgiveness. In many cases this is due to the lack of completion that people expect and want to experience with another human being. Forgiveness is often times overlooked as one's suffering might inspire one to not want anything less for the other. In black and white we can agree that forgiveness is the 'right thing to do' and it is. In fact, all religions practice this fundamental belief. But it doesn't always work this way in practice. Many times people are invested in their emotional body and cannot get beyond the local; there is a need to feel their point was made, justice was served, and the other person needs to suffer just like the rest of us.

This belief system is a part of the mental body resulting from past woundings of the inner child. If we do not address the inner child and attempt to heal these woundings we are more or less unable to forgive others. We literally get stuck in the mental process that is fueled by an exaggerated emotional state. The inner child wants healing; to be forgiven and to forgive. The adult, living with the wounds of the past, often times can not see beyond the pain that is triggered from these childhood events. This is expressed in nonsensical arguments that are difficult to comprehend in the cold light of day. But in the heat of emotional fray, things happen. Many times perfectly adjusted adults will argue over knitting needles, or the thread-count in sheets, or some other ridiculous issue of ego-driven insignificance. Subsequently, they never forgive each other for an argument that didn't make sense to begin with. This is common with family members who carry forever-unresolved issues (often insignificant) from the past. Sometimes, we pick topics that might emanate from current situations of the day, but in reality they are fueled by long-standing painful memories and deep-seated resentment. This pain and resentment goes into the wounds like salt and brings up an immediate response that ignores the present moment but focuses on the past and years of unresolved issues.

HOW YOU WOULD GO ABOUT FORGIVING

The process of forgiveness consists of two things: your intention and your heart.

Visualize the person you want to forgive in front of you and say out loud or in your mind 'I am now forgiving you for any pain or wrongdoing you may have caused me from the time of creation until now and I am asking that all karma be cleared and transmuted up into light and love.'

Visualize the person to whom you are offering forgiveness saying the same thing back to you.

By doing this exercise in the privacy of your home or office and visualizing your family, friends, and people throughout your life, you not only heal your own karma, you create healing for the world.

This is a good thing. We are all connected and by forgiving those who have crossed our paths in this lifetime the ripple effect in the pond goes out far and wide around the world.

FORGIVING MYSELF

The process of forgiving oneself is often the most challenging. We can find all kinds of reasons to beat ourselves up over what we have done, or should have done, or didn't do. The proverbial stick gets bigger as we grow up. Finding reasons why we have failed becomes widespread; this way of looking at life (rather than self love) becomes our common denominator.

When we finally choose to forgive ourselves we often have to wade past the negative sounds of the inner critic in order to find the stop button for that voice that keeps us from healing. The wounded inner child has carried the pain and suffering right into adulthood, accompanied by the voice of the critic.

So how do we forgive ourselves with all of this going on? We must first identify the core of our self-esteem. This concept of self-esteem has many definitions in today's self-help world. I like to look at it from a perspective of healing. Self-esteem means that you have a right to be here as a soul in a body on the earth. When we have fully embraced that statement and implemented it right down into the core of our being we can then move into a place of forgiveness for ourselves, and others.

In order to forgive oneself it is necessary to realize that we have purpose and value in being here on the planet as a soul in a body. The purpose has to do with your right to be here. It is not about what you are or where you went to school or how many badges you have earned. It is simply your right to be here.

To forgive yourself, you must see yourself standing in front of you, or stand looking into a mirror. From a place of intention and heart, tell yourself that you forgive yourself. Reaffirm it by telling yourself that you are loved by you. Say the words "I love you" to yourself. It is that simple.

Try to identify where in your body the pain and suffering resides; that infraction which you created to bring about a reason for forgiveness. See yourself reaching into your body as if that feeling were an object, and allow your hands to envelope it. Witness a healing energy coming out of your hands, dissolving the pain. As it dissolves repeat again to yourself the words—I forgive you and I love you.

A client once got angry with me, saying; "I don't have time to forgive myself; to stand around telling myself that I love myself. I have real problems!"

"Yes you do," I said, "and if you don't start addressing them from the inside-out you will keep running these patterns for the rest of your life!"

I explained to her that it was the wounded inner child that needed to be loved and nurtured. If we take the time to heal the inner child we would be able to tell ourselves that we forgive and love at every turn in the road. We would also have a smoother passage when our death is at hand, given that we are at peace. In this state we are less likely to be consumed with fighting unresolved issues of pain, sadness, neglect, and fear.

TEACHING PEOPLE TO FORGIVE FROM A YOUNG AGE

We can teach our children the process of forgiveness at a very young age. It is the restructuring of a pattern that prevails in many cultures. Forgiveness is kept under lock-and-key within the confines of many religions. We are taught moral standards, love and forgiveness in a theoretical sort of fashion. To make forgiveness a practical daily occurrence that is as common as brushing one's teeth is not something we have yet achieved in our world.

Tell your children that to forgive one another, friends, cousins and parents is a way of helping to heal those people and their own feelings.

Reassure your children that their feelings are valid. They can be held accountable for their actions, but forgiveness is separate and is needed to heal situations.

When they don't want to heal their issues or move past them try to work with their emotional body. Through conversation (or creative art) allow them to express their feelings with the intent that they are going to gain understanding in order to be able to forgive and heal.

It is not constructive to drag them to Aunt Mabel to force them to confess their forgiveness (or to be forgiven). You will find that this approach will rarely work.

Grant them the same dignity that you would want, allowing them to process their issues privately with yourself and/or with a counselor.

It is important that we do not shame our children into practicing this very powerful process that is meant to heal. Very often, I find that people do not want to forgive because they feel they have not been heard, seen, felt, or understood. Understand how your child learns about the world; through their ears (hearing), their eyes (visual), their gut (feeling), their brain (mental process). Discover these learning modalities and help your child learn how to be heard, seen, felt, and understood. Then practice forgiveness yourself as an example to them.

PEOPLE WHO FAILED TO FORGIVE

Sometimes people miss the mark and wait too long to do a process of forgiveness. Tragically, a loved one dies. Then they think there is no chance to make forgiveness with that person because they have crossed over into the spirit realm. I hear from clients regularly who want to be forgiven or to forgive a parent or loved one who has already crossed over.

In readings, I often facilitate such processes of forgiveness and inevitably there are things said from the spirit realm that only my client would know. This brings a level of validation to the client that helps the process even more. Many times people die suddenly and they have not had a chance to forgive or be forgiven. This is not the end of the road; in fact, it is often the beginning. Allowing my abilities as a spiritual intuitive to facilitate gives clarity and relief to both sides.

My favorite story of forgiveness involved a woman who called me from her hospital bed; she was coping with stage-four cancer. Many concerns about her upcoming death troubled her. They included unresolved, painful issues between her and her father. I could see both her parents standing by her bedside and told her so. Here is her story.

"Your father is asking you to forgive him for the pain he has caused in your life."

She cried. She said he had beaten her so bad as a child, but she had not talked about it to anyone. She was finally ready.

"Papa, I forgive you." Healing in that moment resolved a lifetime of pain and suffering. She was comforted to know her parents awaited her and that she had released the emotional bonds of this lifetime.

Ten things to do in your process of forgiveness

Have clear intention to forgive

Be in your heart

Find a quiet place where you will not be interrupted

Get grounded

Visualize the person you want to forgive sitting across from you; use your movie mind

Say the following words: I am now forgiving you for any pain or wrong-doing you may have caused me from the time of creation until now and I am asking that all karma be cleared and transmuted up into light and love

Now visualize that person saying it back to you

Visualize yourself giving them a gift: a rock, a feather, a dove, or a self-help book. Thank them; release them and see them walk away

Tell yourself that you forgive yourself and love yourself

Feel the freedom of your forgiveness as you move through life a little lighter

THE QUALITY OF OUR PASSAGE

The mission statement for humanity is to love at the deepest level of our being. We are meant to love first-and-foremost; to experience love in the physical, mental, emotional and spiritual bodies. All four essential bodies experience love throughout life.

To align the four essential bodies (physical, mental, emotional and spiritual) to a complete state of love takes a great deal of surrender. Surrender is applied to several dispositions. We must surrender the ego, and all attachment to outcomes; we must surrender possessions, people, places and things. In particular we must surrender the ideal of what we think love looks like.

Learn to live more simply, letting go of clutter we insist has value in our lives. This is important.

By living more simply, we would be much more willing to let go of the physical body. Faith tells us we are going to God when all is said and done. This faith, and understanding that we have a higher power, creates balance in divine order. God has our best interest at heart. He is a loving God, not a punitive God. It is only when we choose to be victims to our reality that we create an opening to be that victim. Logic erroneously dictates then that our God is punishing us.

I had to put my mom in a nursing home and I feel guilty all the time. She doesn't understand. When I go visit her she is very angry.

This is not an uncommon situation. This is because she has not had the opportunity to heal her own woundings and is once again experiencing abandonment. This is not to say your decision to have her in a home is wrong. Remember that this is her stuff. View this as her opportunity to look at her emotional body and to feel her feelings.

If she is heavily medicated and/or suffering from dementia, it can be very difficult to reach a place where healing might occur. You can however, offer her comfort. Talk to her inner child; "Mom I brought you a special blanket so you feel safe while you are sleeping."

Very often remembering the past is soothing to people. Talk to her about when she was a child. Ask her to share her stories even if you have heard them a thousand times. She may feel pain in recounting the past and she might express her grief through tears. If this is the case, listen to her. Suggest to her to forgive whomever the story is about, her father or mother. Tell her that it is ok that she feels the feelings now.

Someone your mother's age, who might feel trapped by emotional chains, will need to be set free. We, as family members, can do this for them. Allow her to forgive the people in her life. Ask also that the long passed family members forgive her. Of course they do, but it will give her comfort for you to tell her. That is really all any of us are looking for when we are in pain. To feel comfort and to know we are not alone. We often want others to suffer because we cannot get past our own pain.

In summary, take the time to bring out your mother's stories and help her to forgive the pain and wrongdoing from her past. This will set her free in the emotional body and allow her spiritual body to heal.

Understanding how karma affects our lives helps us claim a new perspective on events. By looking at our relationship to karma and realizing what karmic history we brought into this lifetime we are able to perceive events and experiences from a new perspective. Taking responsibility for one's karma and life lessons is the sign of an evolving soul.

Our karma corresponds to the emotional body where we embrace our feelings. Acknowledging our feelings is the quickest way to move through our past histories. We must be aware; must feel our feelings, processing them with the intention of clearing karma. Beware the ego! It is a trickster; a part of us that refuses to let go, so that he/she can make it into tomorrow's brand new drama.

Forgiveness is crucial. The challenge to the worldly experience of feeling one's feelings, loving to the deepest level of one's being, can be solved through karma. The karmic solution is to forgive. Do we have the courage to face our shortcomings, to forgive ourselves for our human frailties? Yes, we must forgive ourselves. We do this so that we are able to take it one step further; to forgive those who we perceive have wronged us.

We can forgive at that level, even if we have to wrestle the alligator 'ego' keeping it in its place. It is critical to realize that love and forgiveness of another human being is more important than a disagreement, or misunderstanding.

If we do not forgive the people and disagreeable experiences we have had, we tend to come back again and again, lifetime after lifetime trying to heal those very same situations. Let this be a reminder to us—a good reason to end each day with everything said and done. Make sure all is forgiven and we are at peace. This will help us clear our karma and move towards an evolution of our soul's journey. This is enlightenment.

ENLIGHTENMENT

Enlightenment is the goal of the soul's journey through all of these lifetimes we are here on Earth. Enlightenment broadly means wisdom and understanding that enables a clarity of perception. To reach a state of enlightenment one must be surrendered to the knowledge and understanding that we are living in a duality.

DUALITY

Duality is where everything exists, good and bad, dark and light; ever continual contrasts in our lives. The gift of duality is profound. It can become our daily exercise in its observance. It teaches us to relax, not jump in and create situations of extreme highs and lows. Everyone has the ability to observe but not react. Each moment, observed from a new perspective of love, provides the opportunity to grow; to clear karma.

Be responsive. Forgive those around you if they are not being attentive to your needs; not driving, talking, performing, reacting, caring, calling; in other words, not providing you the response you are looking for.

Have no expectations and you will not be let down. Take responsibility for your every moment. Recognize where you might have that characteristic flaw, attitude, prejudice, anger, resentment, or frustration inside of you. Love that part of yourself; be willing to forgive yourself for being that way or having been that way, or ever imagining being that way so that you heal not only yourself, but others as well.

Understanding duality takes time and a daily practice of meditation. There is no greater path to one's own enlightenment than clearing the mind and allowing God's energy to become one with theirs. In essence, you are a part of the God body. It is the experience of being in a physical body that creates separation. This illusion of separation comprises our work on the emotional level. We accomplish this by going through various mini-deaths throughout our lives—separation from mother, friends, college, jobs, marriages, children, parents, and, eventually, our own death.

By stepping back to simply observe that we are merely souls in bodies on the earth, just visitors to this planet, the more we gain perspective on our lives. At the same time, the more we take responsibility for ourselves, recognizing the duality within us we realize the opportunity to heal. We recognize that there is no separation.

All experience is interconnected. Therefore, if we allow this inter-connectedness into our cognitive processes, we can be aware of events independent of all time. But as soon as we say "we" we have fallen back into the dualism. It is hard to experience this connectedness when our major experience of life is duality. Holistic awareness will be outside linear time, outside three-dimensional space and, therefore, will not be easily recognized. We must practice holistic experience to be able to recognize it. Meditation is one way of transcending the limits of the linear mind, allowing the connectedness of all things to become an experiential reality.[12]

BLISS

Reaching a state of enlightenment is connecting with the universe and God on a cellular level. The joy and bliss that is experienced in the spirit realm by loved ones who have passed, is the same joy and bliss one experiences when enlightened in the physical body. Enlightenment is merging the spirit realm and the physical realm with the understanding that time, space, and reality is not what it appears to be. It is the emotional and mental realm one must process and release. The inner work of healing patterns and thought forms that are reflected back to us from others is the key to healing our world.

This work removes us from the role of victim; to being fully responsible to ourselves and others.

I am still feeling waves of sadness and loss since my dad passed away. At times it completely overwhelms me.

The grief process is not something we should miss. The emotional body needs to process the loss and to embrace several stages of grieving in order to assimilate the experience. Our emotional body is attached to the earthly experience, but our spiritual body has a far greater depth of knowledge in this department. We can be comforted by the awareness that our loved ones are with us, around us, and helping us. We can also take comfort in knowing they will be waiting for us when it is our time to cross over. In addition, they will incarnate with us when the family pod is ready to do so. This knowledge allows us space to breath; to release the anxiety we might feel toward our own death.

We can take comfort in recognizing and knowing that those little signs we receive are our loved ones communicating with us -- letting us know they are with us.

The universe is extremely complex and the alignment for each soul in what we have to learn karmically is where we manifest into physical form. The more we move through our karma, clearing the path with forgiveness we move closer to manifesting a conscious state of joy and bliss.

The mission statement for humanity is to love at the deepest level of our being.

The work consists of processing and feeling our feelings.

The karma solution is to love at the deepest level of our being, feel our feelings and forgive (ourselves and others).

Forgiveness is to clear one's karma.

We face the passage as fellow travelers. But that is not the end to it. It isn't over -- we do go on. There is a higher consciousness that participates, celebrates, and loves our every step towards our own self-realization.

GLOSSARY

ASTRAL

Consisting of a supersensible substance held in theosophy to be next above the tangible world in refinement.

ASTRAL PLANE

It is the world of the planetary spheres, crossed by the soul in its astral body on the way to being born and after death, and generally said to be populated by angels, spirits or other immaterial beings.

CLAIRVOYANT

Able to see beyond the range of ordinary perception.

CONSCIOUSNESS

Quality or state of being aware especially of something within oneself: the upper level of mental life of which the person is aware—as contrasted with unconscious processes.

DEATH

Permanent cessation of all vital functions: the end of life.

DESTINY
a predetermined course of events often held to be an irresistible power or agency thought to predetermine events.

DUALITY
Duality consists of a pair of opposites, whereas non-duality is the Middle Way which is between, and which also transcends, these opposites. In the Dhammachakkappavattana-Sutta, the Buddha taught the Middle Way between the extremes of attachment to sense pleasures on the one hand, and self-mortification on the other—the Middle Way between the two being the Noble Eightfold Path leading to Enlightenment. This teaching is a practical application of the central insight of Buddhism.[13]

ENLIGHTENMENT
In Buddhism, a final blessed state marked by the absence of desire or suffering.

GOD
The supreme or ultimate reality: Being perfect in power, wisdom, and goodness that is worshipped as creator and ruler of the universe.

GUARDIAN ANGEL
An angel believed to have special care of a particular individual. A protector.

HEAVEN
A spiritual state of everlasting communion with God: a place or condition of utmost happiness.

INCARNATE
Invested with bodily and especially human nature and form: embodied.

KARMA
The force generated by a person's actions held in Hinduism and Buddhism to perpetuate transmigration and in its ethical consequences to determine the nature of the person's next existence.

KINESTHETIC
Sensory experience derived from physical movement.

MENTAL
Relating to the total emotional and intellectual response of an individual to external reality: intellectual as contrasted with emotional or physical activity.

MANIFEST
Readily perceived by the senses and especially by the sight: easily understood or recognized by the mind.

PASSAGE
The action or process of passing from one place, condition, or stage to another: death.

REINCARNATION
Rebirth in new bodies or forms of life: a rebirth of a soul in a new human body.

SOUL
The immaterial essence, animating principle, or actuating cause of an individual life: the spiritual principle embodied in human beings.

UNIVERSE
The world of human experience: the entire celestial cosmos.

VIRGIN MARY
Mother of Jesus.

VICTIMIZE
To make a victim of.

VISUAL
Producing mental images: done or executed by sight only.

REFERENCES

1 Religious perspectives of death by Mike Vines. Retrieved October 2009 from http://www.pioneerthinking.com/mv_death.html

2 Encyclopedia of Death and Dying. Retrieved October 2009 from http://www.deathreference.com/A-Bi/African-Religions.html

3 National Aeronautics and Space Administration. Retrieved October 2009 from http://www.nasa.gov/

4 Elizabeth Kubler-Ross, quoted in Energy Medicine, Donna Eden, op. cit., (1998)

5 Donna Eden, (1998). Energy Medicine, Tarcher/Putnam, New York. p. 207.

6 Encyclopedia of Death and Dying. Retrieved October 2009 from http://www.deathreference.com/Py-Se/Reincarnation.html

7 Wikipedia. Retrieved October 2009 from http://en.wikipedia.org/wiki/Consciousness

8 Stanford Encyclopedia of Philosophy. Retrieved October 2009 from http://en.wikipedia.org/wiki/Destiny

9 Wikipedia. Retrieved October 2009 from http://en.wikipedia.org/wiki/Neuro-linguistic_programming#Concepts_and_methods

10 Wikipedia. Retrieved October 2009 from http://www.deathreference.com/Py-Se/Reincarnation.html

11 From Latin, meaning, "it's a wonder to relate."

12 Barbara Ann Brennan, (1988). Hands of Light. Pleiades Books by Bantam

13 The Doctrine of Non Duality in the Vimalakirti Nirdesa Sutra

OTHER BOOKS BY EDUCARE PRESS
Available on the web

HONEY BUN BY ANNE STOCKTON

Honey-Bun is a simple, personal memoir of the author, who uses the death of her cat as a vehicle for examining life and loss. Author Anne Stockton invites us to examine the unique relationship between animals and people. After the death of her much-loved cat, Stockton finds solace in her ability to explore their past together. Through words, art and philosophy, we begin to understand how the pain of losing a beloved companion can bring us closer to an understanding of our entire lives and lead to a glorious rebirth. Narrated by Stockton's remarkable pastels, Honey-Bun is not only a touching tribute, but also a work of art.

The author

Sonja Grace travels around the world presiding over her gallery group venue called **Sonja Grace in the Circle**. Sonja delivers important, clear information from her guides and answers questions from the audience. She offers workshops that provide a positive grounded platform to discover and enable many levels of healing. Sonja does phone readings for clients around the globe.

"Time and space are not what we perceive them to be," she reveals.

Sonja is able to provide healing in the physical, mental, emotional and spiritual bodies. She lives with her husband and two cats in Portland, Oregon.

www.sonjagrace.com

CPSIA information can be obtained at www.ICGtesting.com
Printed in the USA
BVOW08s1723220114

342685BV00002B/416/P